THE PREVAILING POWER OF FASTING

Festus Adeyeye

THE PREVAILING POWER OF FASTING

Copyright © 2015 by Festus Adeyeye

Printed in the United States of America. All rights reserved solely by the author. No part of this book may be reproduced in any form without the written permission of the author.

Unless otherwise indicated, Bible quotations are taken from King James Version. Copyright © 1988 by B. B. Kirkbride Bible Company. Encarta world English dictionary 1998 - 2004 Microsoft Corporation.

ISBN 13: 978-1-944652-07-4

FORMATTED AND PRINTED BY:

Triumph Publishing
P. O. Box 690158
Bronx, New York 10469
www.triumphpublishing.net
718-652-7157

ORDERING INFORMATION:

To order books, Cds and DVDs by Dr. Festus Adeyeye, please write to:

Dr. Festus Adeyeye
Adeyeye Evangelistic Ministries (AEM)
P.O Box 810
West Hempstead, NY 11552
e-mail: aboluade@aol.com
website: www.alccwinnershouse.org

DEDICATION

This book is dedicated to God for giving me the anointing, wisdom and boldness to write another book to His loved ones.

This book is also dedicated to my wife, who is also my friend and partner in ministry, **Pastor Anthonia Adeyeye**. Your love, commitment and sacrifices are unparalleled. Thank you.

To my children: **Blessing, Joy, Emmanuel, Faith** and **Phillip**: Thank you for your prayers and support. I love you all.

To **Jide, Lola, Vicky** and **Tope Ajifowobaje**: for being part of my life and family. Thanks for your love and support.

To my maternal grandmother, late **Julie Alabi**: for imparting wisdom, discipline and good work ethics to me during my early years.

ACKNOWLEDGEMENTS

I thank the Almighty God for transforming my life and the lives of others, through me. I love you God and I will forever be grateful for your love and presence upon my life.

I thank the leaders and members of **Abundant Life Christian Center Worldwide**. You continue to believe in me and have stood firmly and prayerfully behind the call of God in my life. To all ALCC intercessors, you are appreciated. As you help to interpret this great commission, the "I AM THAT I AM" will cause you to be fulfilled in life and will raise men and women to interpret your visions.

I will forever be grateful to God for these men and women whose teachings, writings and invaluable advice have truly encouraged me: Late **Kenneth E. Hagin, Reverend A.R. Bernard, Bishop David Oyedepo, Bishop I.V. & Dr. Bridget Hilliard, Reverend Blessed Nwobiocha**, and my first Pastor, late **Reverend Owenanse;** thank God for using you to raise me up as an intercessor in my formative years at **Oke-Ado Assemblies of God Church**, Ibadan, Nigeria.

Special thanks to my Editorial Team:

Titilola Akinyemi, Editor-in-Chief; **Bukola Akeredolu** and **Deacon Sam Adelusimo**, Proofreader and Editorial Adviser, for their ceaseless efforts and labor in the completion of this book. May God richly reward and bless all of you.

CONTENTS

Introduction — 9

Chapter One
No one can do it for you — 13

Chapter Two
Fasting for a Change — 25

Chapter Three
Engaging in Acceptable Fast for Maximum Benefits — 41

Chapter Four
The Rewards of Fasting (What happens when you fast) — 51

Chapter Five
Fasting, A Divine Booster in Knowing the Will of God — 67

Chapter Six
The Role of Prayer in Fasting — 81

Chapter Seven
Daily Prayer Guide for Morning and Evening Devotion — 89

Chapter Eight
Proofs of Prevailing Prayers — 109

INTRODUCTION

In November 2009, as I was meditating on our ministry's upcoming 2010 annual 21 days of fasting and prayers, I heard the Spirit of the Lord say to me, "Write a book on fasting to prepare and empower my people for an undefeatable journey into the New Year."

It is very important that you don't step into any new day, new week, new month or any new year and expect it to be like previous ones. Each day, each week, each month and each year carries with it, specific divine allocations from God for your life. His mercies are new every morning and He daily loads us with benefits. As you press forward in the journey of life, there must be an insatiable hunger of faith inside of your soul to tap into and embrace all that heaven has apportioned for your life. There must also be a holy anger to reject and terminate hell's entire manifesto concerning you. We live in an era of power! Nothing functions in the earthly realm without a source of power, be it biological, biochemical, electrical or mechanical. A man's destiny soars high through spiritual power, so until you are empowered spiritually, your destiny is at risk.

> *And he said, Thy name shall be called no more Jacob, but Israel: for as a prince hast thou power with God and with men, and hast prevailed.*
> *Genesis 32:28*

Prior to the encounter above, Jacob used all manner of human schemes in an attempt to leverage the power of men. Every attempt failed until he prevailed with God. When you connect with the power of God, you will command power with men. Fasting is one of the avenues for gaining such power with God and ultimately with men. *"Thy name shall be called no more Jacob."* Are there any unnecessary weights of destiny that you are carrying contrary to God's plan for your life? Or do you bear identities that are contrary to God's plan for your life? This is the hour to contact power like Jacob did so you can break away from such weights and identities into a life of dignity and freedom. As you prevail in fasting and prayer as prescribed in this book, I see you enter into your total freedom, in Jesus name!

During a divine visitation in the early hours of March 7, 1999, God said to me, "I am sending you to my people to liberate them from the oppression of ignorance and darkness." This book contains simple but vital spiritual insights that will spark an unquenchable fire inside of you to enjoy a life of fruitfulness, dominion and supernatural exploits, as you grow in your kingdom walk. Jesus Christ paid the price for our redemption and dominion; however, we need to stand firm on the authority of His finished work.

Woe to them that are at ease in Zion, and trust in the mountain of Samaria, which are named chief of the nations, to whom the house of Israel came. Amos 6:1

INTRODUCTION

Many people have taken their Christian journey too easy; no wonder they have been eased out of the abundant life in Christ. Engaging yourself in a lifestyle of fasting coupled with prayer, positions you to ride above every satanic assault. May you enjoy rest in the midst of storms and experience breakthrough in the face of adversity.

Chapter One

NO ONE CAN DO IT FOR YOU

CHAPTER ONE

NO ONE CAN DO IT FOR YOU

Just like no one can use his or her lungs to breath for you, so also no one can be empowered for you. Everyone needs personal empowerment for personal fulfillment.

> *Then all those virgins arose, and trimmed their lamps. And the foolish said unto the wise, give us of your oil, for our lamps are gone out. But the wise answered saying, not so; lest there be not enough for us and for you, but go ye rather to them that sell AND BUY FOR YOURSELVES.*
> Matthew 25:7-9

The five foolish Virgins in the above scriptures did not understand this principle of personal empowerment. They went to the other five wise Virgins expecting them to do for them what they should have done for themselves. To avoid running out of oil needed for the race of life, everyone must go to where it is available and purchase it. Spiritual empowerment is a personal adventure that every person must be willing to embark upon. It is not just for a few or just for some class of people; it is for all. *"The law and the Prophets were until John: since that time the kingdom of God is preached, and every man presses into it."* (Luke 16:16). Spiritual empowerment demands personal pressing through the discipline of fasting, coupled with effective prayer.

THE SECRET IS IN THE SECRET

The secret to being powerful in the public is to be powerful in your secret. Many are weak in their secret and want to be powerful in the public. This has led to the demise of great potentials and great minds. It has led to the demise of great leaders and great dynasties and empires. In order to command power in the public, you must be willing to be strong in your secret. Jesus performed several miracles daily in the open; however, He spent most of his private life in the presence of God on the mountain. His public ministry was an outflow of the abundance of His discipline and fellowship with His father in the secret. There is nothing that empowers a man for public command of power and influence like gaining mastery over himself in the secret. Effective fasting, coupled with prayers, is that personal spiritual discipline engaged upon in the secret that confers public authority.

In my book, *"Pathways to Breakthrough,"* I wrote that Adam and Eve's disobedience of eating the forbidden fruit was the original cause of man losing his God-given dominion in the Garden of Eden. Christ restored man's dominion by fasting forty days and forty nights in the wilderness, overcoming the fiercest attacks of the enemy. (Luke 4:1-13). Adam and Eve were given the Garden of

Eden as their home, with the instructions that they could partake freely of the fruit in the Garden - except fruits on the Tree of Knowledge of Good and Evil.

So when the woman saw that the tree was good for food, that it was pleasant to the eyes, and a tree desirable to make one wise, she took of the fruit and ate. She also gave to her husband with her, and he ate. Genesis 3:6

This single act of disobedience by Adam and Eve ushered sin and sorrow into the world for themselves and for the entire human race.

Christ, the last Adam refused to succumb to temptation. Instead of succumbing to the devil's suggestion of creating and eating bread, Jesus continued and completed His fasting. By so doing, He won back that which was lost by Adam and Eve. Jesus broke through! The first Adam failed by eating but the last Adam (Christ) was victorious by abstaining from food.

THE DISCIPLINE OF THE APPETITE

It is true that lack of discipline over the appetites of the flesh can lead to spiritual barrenness and even disaster. Fasting, which is the act of refraining from food and other pleasures of life, has the opposite effect; it gives men a new grip on God. Esau's downfall was similar to Adam and Eve's; he sold his birthright for a bite of food.

And Jacob said; Sell me this day thy birthright. And Esau said, Behold, I am at the point to die: and what profit shall this birthright do to me? And Jacob said, Swear to me this day; and he swore unto him: and he sold his birthright unto Jacob. Then Jacob gave Esau bread and pottage of lentils; and he did eat and drink, and rose up, and went his way: thus Esau despised his birthright.
Genesis 25:31-33

By gratifying his appetite, Esau forfeited the glory that could have been his. Many have lost the battle for a glorious marriage, a glorious destiny, and a glorious ministry because they could not discipline themselves in fasting and prayer. This is more prevalent in the developed countries where there is much comfort and ease and an abundance of food.

Many cannot break through in their health because of excessive eating of hormonally grown foods. It is medically proven that fasting is good for your health. The discipline of the soul that comes from abstaining from the earthly pleasures of life opens the door to the heavenlies. Again and again in the scripture, we find people losing their divine placements in God through failure to control the appetites of the flesh. At the same time, we find other examples of people who through the discipline of fasting, overcame all obstacles and obtained answers from God that changed the destinies of kingdoms.

By lusting for the delicacies of Egypt, the Israelites lost the blessings of God.

> *They lusted exceedingly in the wilderness, and tested God in the desert. And he gave them their request, but sent leanness into their soul.*
> *Psalm 106:14, 15*

But their leader, Moses through intercession and fasting for forty days, saved them from destruction as a nation. Those living in Noah's days were so given over to satisfying their appetites that they were unaware of the gathering clouds of judgment until suddenly they found themselves being carried away in the flood.

> *But as the days of Noah were so shall also the coming of the Son of man be. For as in the days that were before the flood they were eating and drinking, marrying and giving in marriage, until the day that Noah entered into the ark.*
> *Matthew 24: 37-38*

Jesus warned his disciples not to be like those who lived in the days of Noah. He told them that through fasting and prayer done in faith, they would be able to overcome the powers of evil and cast out demons.

> *Then came the disciples to Jesus apart and said, why could not we cast him out? And Jesus said unto them, because of your unbelief: for verily I say unto you, If ye have faith as a grain of mustard*

> seed, ye shall say unto this mountain, remove hence to yonder place; and it shall remove; and nothing shall be impossible unto you. Howbeit this kind goes not out but by prayer and fasting.
> Matt. 17:19-21

Failures in the past may have been many, but fasting will win the battle and put the enemy to flight. When Israel lost two great battles and was humbled to the dust by the tragic loss of thousands of lives, her people fasted and wept before the Lord. The next day their defeat was turned into victory. Judges 20.

The Scripture is very clear concerning the subject of fasting. Jesus was very specific and instructive regarding fasting. Jesus taught on three essential covenant practices in Matthew Chapter 6. These covenant practices are: prayer, giving and fasting. He started his teachings on each of them with "when thou" and not with "if thou."

"Therefore when thou doest thy alms..."
Matthew 6:2

"But when thou pray..." Matthew 6:6

"When ye fast..." Matthew 6:17

Giving, praying and fasting are not optional but divine covenant practices of the believer. Fasting is not a dispensational doctrine that ends with an era of Christianity but rather a divine exercise set by God for believers to disarm the assaults of hell. If you don't want the devil to deprogram and disconnect you from God's agenda, it is better for you to plug yourself into the divine program of fasting set by God for His people. The devil and the flesh make it uncomfortable for some believers to fast because fasting is the only way to disarm Satan's agenda and to subdue the hold of flesh on any life.

THE ERA OF FASTING AND NOT FEASTING:

A question arose one day as the Scribes and the Pharisees observed Jesus and his disciples eating with publicans and sinners. "Why do the disciples of John and of the Pharisees fast, but thy disciples fast not?" And Jesus answered them thus:

> *Can the children of the bridechamber fast, while the bridegroom is with them? As long as they have the bridegroom with them, they cannot fast. But the days will come when the bridegroom shall be taken away from them, and then shall they fast in those days. Mark 2:19-20.*

According to the insight given to us by our Savior Jesus Christ in the above scripture, the followers of Christ will engage in fasting when he is no longer present physically with them. Since Jesus, the bridegroom is no more on the earth in bodily form, it is then scripturally accurate to say that we are in the era of fasting. When Jesus who was a type of bridegroom was bodily present on the earth, he provided such a heavy supernatural covering for his disciples that could not be penetrated by the host of hell. He gave direction and made provisions for their ministry that they did not need to engage in any fast. If you are invited to a restaurant for a wedding reception, it is expected that you will eat without paying for the food. However you cannot go back to the same restaurant and expect to eat free after the wedding ceremony is over and the bridegroom is gone.

Jesus has risen and is seated at the right hand of majesty. Although he still provides heavier covering and provisions for believers from his exalted position in the heavenly places, his disciples cannot continue to engage in feasting but rather in fasting as a lifestyle. As a believer, fasting is not optional. It is not "if I should fast" but rather "when I fast." Fasting is to be part of my covenant walk with God on the earth in order to fulfill my divine assignment. Fasting should not be a legalistic and ritualistic form of lifestyle but a spiritual covenant practice motivated by love and initiated by the power of the Holy Spirit. This is the reason I come in the volume of these pages to ignite an unquenchable fire of power inside of your soul in the mighty name of Jesus Christ! On another occasion Jesus told His disciples about "this kind" of issues; Jesus said,

> "... *This kind goes not out but by prayer and fasting." Matthew 17:21*

Jesus made it known here in clear terms what it takes to command power in order to terminate the assault of hell in any life. These kinds are more prevalent today than any other time. Satan has a very limited time and he is unleashing the best of his wickedness on the human race. There are "these kinds" of forces arrayed against you and me that demand praying and fasting. The bible says in 2nd Peter 5:9, *"Whom resist steadfast…"*

Biblical fasting coupled with the prayer of faith is one of the keys to resisting the onslaught of the enemy over a destiny. Beware of the contentions on your birthright and remain properly positioned for it. Some were genuinely called but were not ready for the cost and they lost their callings. You have been called unto glory and virtue but you must be ready for the cost in order to give expression to the glory.

The quality of your spiritual investment is what determines your ultimate accomplishment in life. Spiritual exercise is useful and of value in everything and in every way, 1st Timothy 4:8b (Amplified). Fasting is indeed a profitable spiritual investment.

> *Be not deceived, God is not mocked: for whatsoever a man sows that shall he also reap. For he that sows to his flesh shall of the flesh reap corruption: but he that sows to the Spirit shall of the Spirit reap life everlasting. Galatians 6:7-8*

Chapter Two

FASTING FOR A CHANGE

CHAPTER TWO

FASTING FOR A CHANGE

My wife and I have seen our destinies transformed by the power of God through the discipline of fasting. We continue to enjoy unprecedented favor and blessings of God in our lives and ministry that can not be attributed to any man but to God's response to a lifestyle of fasting. The supernatural power of God is made manifest daily in our ministry, changing the landscape of the lives of multitudes to the glory of God.

Irrespective of the verdict of the enemy over your life, it can be changed through fasting. There was a conspiracy by Haman to destroy the entire Jewish people in Shushan. The price was paid and the King approved of the plot.

> *And the king took his ring from his hand, and gave it unto Haman the Agagite, the Jewish enemy. And the king said unto Haman, the silver is given to thee, the people also to do with them, as it seems good to thee. Esther 3:10-11*

However Esther rose up to the challenge in fasting. God changed the verdict; Haman's conspiracy was shattered. The sentence was reversed and Haman himself was destroyed in the gallows he built for the extermination of the Jewish people.

> *Go gather together all the Jews that are present in Shushan, and fast ye for me, and neither eat nor drink three days, night or day: I also and my maidens will fast likewise: and so will I go in unto the King which is not according to the law and if I perish, I perish. Esther 4:16.*

There is a devil seating on your inheritance that must be unseated. There is a resister of destiny wanting to resist your destiny that must be resisted. He is the adversary seeking whom to devour. He can wreak great havoc if left unchecked. But thank God that we have the redemptive authority in Christ to resist and stop him as we hold steadfast in faith. You can terminate all his conspiracies concerning your destiny. Fasting is one of your divine ammunitions for accomplishing this task. It is a divine program that guarantees your triumph in the race of life. Through the discipline of fasting, we see examples of men like Apostle Paul who contacted heaven to prevail against the raging forces of nature. Apostle Paul gained victory over the raging storm on the ocean that would have killed him with the two hundred and seventy seven men that were on board with him. Paul provoked heaven and secured divine intervention that subdued the raging forces of the storm. Paul's life was preserved with that of everyone inside the ship! He was able to rest in the midst of the storm.

> *But after long fasting, Paul stood forth in the midst of them and said, Sirs, you should have hearkened unto me and not have sailed from Crete, and to have gained this harm and loss and now I exhort you to be of good cheer: for there shall be no loss of any man's life among you but of the ship. For there stood by me this night the angel of God whose I am and whom I serve, saying fear not Paul: thou must be brought before Caesar, and lo God has given thee all that sail with thee.*
> *Acts 27:21-24*

You can also subdue every storm-like situation that constitutes a threat to your life and that of your family. There are certain dimensions of change you seek from God that will require you to embark on long fasting in order to provoke your miracle harvest.

Another example was Daniel who through the prevailing power of fasting pierced through the demonic atmosphere ruling over his nation. He gained access to the mind of God regarding the destiny of his people, Israel.

> *In those days I Daniel was mourning three full weeks. I ate no pleasant bread, neither came flesh nor wine in my mouth, neither did I anoint myself at all, till three whole weeks were fulfilled.*
> *Daniel 10:2-3*

Vs: 14. Now I am come to make thee understand what shall befall thy people in the latter days: for yet the vision is for many days.

Are you groping in the dark concerning certain issues in your life? You can also receive the light of heaven's revelation that will give you an inside information. Such inside information when believed will cause you to experience rest where others are losing their minds. My God is an unchanging God. Whatsoever He did for His people then, He will still do today in response to anyone who will by faith lift up the altar of fasting and stand upon the authority of God's word. No matter the raging fire of the enemy confronting your life, you can turn the tides around. I challenge you today to stop waiting for the change you desire but to launch into the deep and take up the armor of God in fasting to provoke the change.

WHAT IS BIBLICAL FASTING?

According to the Webster New Ideal Dictionary, fasting is to abstain from food; to eat sparingly or abstain from some foods. Scripturally speaking, fasting is a conscious, intentional decision to abstain for a time from the pleasure of eating to gain vital spiritual benefits. It is chastening the flesh to free up our spirits to focus on and receive from God. Dan. 9:2-10. Fasting is a covenant practice initiated by God both in the old and new testaments for his people. It is a spiritual exercise of abstaining from food in order to focus on God and the things of God. Fasting is clearly different from dieting or hunger strikes. Biblical and acceptable fasting is to intentionally refrain from food for Godly spiritual purpose. It is abstaining from food so we can stay with God. Abstaining from food does not make your fasting beneficial; staying with God does.

DIFFERENT KINDS OF FASTS:

There are three types of fasting known in the scriptures. However, I must warn that you must not be dogmatic or legalistic as to what form of fast to engage in. God is very mindful of where you are in order to get you ready for where He is taking you.

According to your ability:

And unto one he gave five talents, to another two, and to another one: TO EVERYMAN ACCORDING TO HIS SEVERAL ABILITIES. Matthew 25: 15

If any man speaks let him speak as the oracles of God. If any man ministers, let him do it as of the ability which God gives: that God in all things may be glorified through Jesus Christ, to whom be praise and dominion for ever and ever Amen.
1st Peter 4:11

God has given to everyman some definite level of ability to obey him. You are to recognize your own level of ability in cooperation with the Holy Spirit to know the type of fasting to embark upon. Just as you grow in faith, you can also grow in the level of your ability to fast. Fasting must be done in faith and under the leadership of the Holy Spirit.

Absolute Fast:

This is abstinence from food and water. There are several examples of this in the scripture. Queen Esther engaged in this type of fast for 3 days when Haman conspired to destroy all the Jews in Shushan.

> *Go gather together all the Jews that are present in Shushan, and fast ye for me, and neither eat nor drink three days, night or day: I also and my maidens will fast likewise: and so will I go in unto the King which is not according to the law and if I perish, I perish. Esther 4:16*

Another example was when Saul of Tarsus encountered Jesus on the road to Damascus and changed his name to Paul, also changing his destiny and assignment.

> *And Saul arose from the earth: and when his eyes were opened he saw no man. But they led him by the hand, and brought him into Damascus. And he was three days without sight, and neither did eat nor drink. Acts 9:8-9*

Other examples under this category were the 40 days and 40 nights fast of Elijah and Moses. I believe the two scenarios of supernatural fast of Moses and Elijah should not be used as examples but rather as exceptions.

> *And Moses was there with the Lord forty days and forty nights; he did neither eat bread, nor drink water. And he wrote upon the tables the words of the covenant, the Ten Commandments.*
> *Exodus 34:28.*

This is because the scripture prior to this says God appeared to Moses. The glory of God was there, and Moses was caught up in it. Imagine being in the presence of God wrapped up in His glory, I bet anyone will lose all sense of time. The forty days must have seemed like 40 seconds to Moses. I am convinced that no one will remember food or be hungry in the presence of the almighty God, no matter the length of time.

Look at what the bible says about the case of Elijah,

> *"And the angel of the Lord came again the second time and touched him, and said, Arise and eat; because the journey is too great for thee."*
> *1st Kings 19:7.*

If an angel came down and fed you, you might be able to go for many months in the strength of that divine menu. Even though I am of the opinion that this type of fast is not impossible but you must strictly be led by God. I do engage in long fasting but not without water, as discussed in the next type of fasting below. And if you are led of God to embark on such long fasting without water and food, God will surely grace you to accomplish it.

Partial Fast:

Daniel fasted 21 days and ate no "pleasant bread." Daniel didn't eat anything he wanted; he cut down on his menu. He had an adjustment on his diet for three weeks.

> *In those days I, Daniel was mourning three full weeks. I ate no pleasant bread, neither came flesh nor wine in my mouth, neither did I anoint myself at all, till three whole weeks were fulfilled.*
> *Daniel 10:2-3*

It was recorded that John Wesley (founder of the Methodist Church) lived mostly on dry bread diet. He lived in the realm of God's power and anointing to impart many generations. This form of fasting could be skipping a meal and it is appropriate for elderly people. This is paying some price of inconvenience or discomfort in order to attain the comfort of the Holy Spirit.

Normal Fast:

This is the third and the last type of fast. When you engage in a long fast and live on water only, you are engaging in a normal fast. We see this example in Jesus Christ's fast in the wilderness.

> *Being forty days tempted of the devil. And in those days he did eat nothing; and when they were ended, he afterward hungered. Luke 4:2*

He was afterward hungered and not afterward thirsty. I remember reading an unknown author commenting on this scripture; I want to concur with his comment and adopt it as my personal opinion. In this scripture, the bible says, Jesus hungered not that He thirsted for water. I want to ASSUME that he drank water but He did not eat any food. Some other person might say, but where did He get water in the wilderness? As said and written, it is my opinion that when you embark on 'NORMAL' fast it is advisable that you drink water. Medical practitioners support the notion that when you are abstaining from food, pesticides and toxins already stored in our bodies must be flushed out. The bible says, "My people perish for lack of knowledge" Many well-meaning children of God died too early and prematurely to be with God because they did not apply wisdom and practical precautions in the way and manner they fasted. Child of God, the choice is yours to do as you are led when you do normal fasting.

As I mentioned at the beginning of this chapter, God has graced every one with the ability to obey him. To those who may ask what kind of fast to embark upon, I will ask you to plug in at your own level of ability as led by the Spirit of the living God that lives inside of you. *"That God in all things may be glorified through Jesus*

Christ" (1st Timothy 4:1b). The glory is unto God and not for any man to brag on his ability to fast. Don't fall into the error of comparing yourself with another person. Your ability to embark on any form of fasting above another person should not be seen as evidence of superior spirituality.

The Pharisee stood and prayed thus with himself. God, I thank thee that I am not as other men are; extortioners, unjust, adulterers or even as this publican.

> *I fast twice in the week. I give tithes of all that I possess. And the publican standing afar off would not lift up so much his eyes unto heaven, but smote upon his breast, saying, God be merciful to me a sinner. I tell you, this man went down to his house justified rather than the other. For every one that exalts himself shall be abased; and he that humbles himself shall be exalted. Luke 18:11-14*

We are also never to become dogmatic or legalistic in fasting. It should be entered into as a form of worship borne out of a loving heart to God as led by the Holy Spirit. You are never to rely on the leadings of your human feelings. Your feelings, which are under the control of the flesh, will hardly ever want to embark on fasting. As a matter of fact, fasting helps you to bring your feelings under control. There are times you will sense the grace to embark on fasting and there are times you won't sense the grace. The key is to be led by the Holy Spirit. Considering the different types of fastings available, no one should have any excuse to avoid fasting. You can plug in to either partial, absolute of normal fast. Whatever you are led to do by God, He will grace you to do it.

BE PREPARED
(Preparation Before a Fast)

Life is a matter of preparation. Unprepared people cannot experience the prepared blessings that God has ordained for them.

Thus the kingdom of heaven is likened unto ten Virgins, which took their lamps, and went forth to meet the bridegroom. And five of them were wise, and five were foolish. They that were foolish took their lamps and TOOK NO OIL with them; But the wise TOOK OIL in their vessels with their lamps.

> *Vs. 8 And the foolish said unto the wise, Give us of your oil; FOR OUR LAMPS ARE GONE OUT. Matthew 25:1-4, 8*

One of the lessons from the above scriptures is that the five foolish virgins were not adequately prepared to meet the bridegroom. They took no oil with them. The oil is a type of the anointing. They entered the journey of life without proper preparation to get to the finish line. Even though the goal was for them to meet with the bridegroom but because of lack of preparation, they missed out on what destiny ordained for them. I set myself in agreement with you that from henceforth you will adequately position yourself to receive what destiny has packaged for you in Jesus name.

There is the need for us to be prepared spiritually, mentally, emotionally and physically in order to receive the manifestation of what God has prepared for us, especially before embarking on a fast.

When the Israelites were to cross over river Jordan to possess Jericho, God instructed Joshua to be prepared spiritually and mentally. Joshua 1:1-9. God told Joshua to be well positioned for the divine assignment. He was told to meditate on the Word of God and to be strong and courageous. If you are going to embrace all that God has for you, you must courageously believe and act on the Word of God. Not only was Joshua instructed to be well prepared and positioned for the next level, the Israelites were also instructed to do the same.

> *Then Joshua commanded the officers of the people, saying, Pass through the host, and command the people, saying, PREPARE you victuals; for within three days ye shall pass over this Jordan, to go in to POSSESS THE LAND. Joshua 1:10-11*

Some of the things that can cause us to be unprepared are:

a) Un-confessed Sin
b) Unbelief
c) Wrong Association(s)
d) Ignorance

e) Fear
f) Slothfulness
g) Procrastination

Make every effort to rid yourself of any of the issues mentioned above so you can embrace the best of God through your fast.

- Before you embark on any type of fast, always set a date and a time for it.

- Establish the purpose for the fast and write down your prayer requests.

- Make sure you always prepare by praying ahead. Ask the Holy Spirit to give you the discipline and enablement needed for the fast. The fact that you have fasted in the past should never cause you to place any confidence in your flesh or on your human ability. You must always ask for the supernatural grace to carry it out with ease. You need to also pray that God should set your focus on spiritual things and not on when to break the fast or with what to break your fast.

Chapter Three

ENGAGING IN AN ACCEPTABLE FAST FOR MAXIMUM BENEFITS

CHAPTER THREE

ENGAGING IN AN ACCEPTABLE FAST FOR MAXIMUM BENEFITS

Why have we fasted, they say and you do not see it? Why have we afflicted ourselves and you take no knowledge of it. Isaiah 58:3a (Amplified)

In order to maximize the benefits of fasting, we need to follow God's order and prescriptions. Many are engaged in fasting without the correspondent blessings from God due to lack of understanding on how to engage in an acceptable fast. There are right reasons and also wrong reasons for fasting:

1. Fasting is not done so you can lose weight. Even though weight loss automatically comes with a prolonged fast, seeking the face of God should be your focus. However, if you fast without prayer and studying of God's word, it is just a physical exercise. I have had a fasting exercise where I lost 30 pounds over a short period of time. I did not step on any weighing scale or even thought once about my weight throughout the fast. My entire focus was on God, His word and intense praying. It was obvious to all at a point that I was up to something as a result of the weight loss. Many

asked me questions as to whether anything was wrong with me. Some thought I was on a special diet or something else. I did not bother to provide any answer because it is a personal discipline. It was after the fast that I weighed myself on scale at home to actually determine the weight loss. I didn't go into fasting with the intention of losing weight but it was a by-product of the fasting.

2. You don't embark on a fast to impress people or show off your spirituality. You are not to go about broadcasting to people that you are engaged in a fast.

Moreover, when ye fast, be not, as the hypocrites, of a sad countenance: for they disfigure their faces that they may appear unto men to fast. Verily I say unto you. They have their reward. But thou when thou fast, anoint thy head, and wash thy face. That thou appear not unto men to fast, but unto thy Father which is in secret: and thy Father, which sees in secret, shall reward thee openly. Matthew 6:16-18.

However, in case of a corporate fast, it is not a sin that your fast is known. The bible also admonished married couples in 1st Corinthians 7:5 to seek the consent of each other in fasting. This is simply because you are not to engage in any form of sexual pleasure during the fasting exercise. It is therefore not sinful for your spouse to know that you are in a fast. In fact, there should be agreement between the two of you before embarking on fasting.

3. Fasting must not be done so God can accept you or to look unto you to have pity on you. Redemption through the finished work of Jesus Christ on the cross is the gateway to your acceptance in the beloved. You and I are forgiven of our sins, accepted by God and have favor with Him based on the blood of the new covenant shed by Jesus Christ. However, fasting will make your spirit sensitive so that you can decipher the sinful areas of your life that need repentance.

THE RIGHT REASONS FOR FASTING

Fast to seek the face of God and not for things (Ministering to the Lord)

The period of fasting should be absolutely dedicated to seeking to know God more than ever before. They that wait upon the Lord shall renew their strength, not they that abstain from food. Ministering to the Lord in fasting is the foundation for an acceptable fast.

> *As they ministered to the Lord, and fasted, the Holy Ghost said, separate me Barnabas and Saul for the work whereunto I have called them.*
> *Acts 13:2*

Take time out to minister to God in songs, in prayer and in the study of His words. Seek to know Him, seek to please Him and seek to love Him more than ever before. Develop an intimacy with Him through a heart-felt fellowship. The focus of a fast should not be to just receive things but rather to seek the face of God. Fasting for things is an elementary form of fasting.

> *And there was also a prophetess, Anna, the daughter of Phanuel, of the tribe of Asher. She was very old, having lived with her husband seven years from her maidenhood. And as a widow even for eighty-four years. She did not go out from the temple enclosure, but was worshipping God night and day with fasting and prayer. Luke 2:36-37 (Amplified)*

Cut off every form of distractions such as excessive conversations with people. I must emphasize the need for this in an age of information technology (Internet, mobile phones, twitters, face book, etc.). The time of fasting is not when to saturate yourself with the mindset of men but rather to gain God's perspective regarding your life. Your spirit man becomes sensitive and alert to the things of the Spirit of God during fasting. You are able to hear God clearly but when you keep calling people, you will miss His call. Also, you need to cease watching television - even Christian channels, so you can focus on seeking God.

ENGAGING IN AN ACCEPTABLE FAST FOR MAXIMUM BENEFITS

> *Ye shall seek me and find me when ye seek me with all your heart. Jeremiah 29:13*

Seekers are finders. What you seek is what you find. And what you behold is also what you become.

> *But we all with open face beholding as in a glass the glory of the Lord are changed into the same image from glory to glory, even by the Spirit of the Lord. 2Corinthians 3:18*

Set time apart to behold God in His word. Fasting without feasting on the Word of God is unprofitable. *"Seek ye first the kingdom of God and its righteousness and all these things shall be added unto you." Matthew 6:13*. When you seek God you will find gold, but when you seek gold, you miss God.

Fasting does not only deliver things to you, it puts you in command of things. Instead of praying just for things, get into God's presence and pray to gain the command of things. Every defeat in life is as a result of not knowing what to do. It is as a result of loss of control and command. The cheapest way to victory is gaining the command of things and having things under control. Fasting with the focus of seeking the presence of God puts you in practical command of issues confronting your life. Even when the situation is not yet changed, there is a grace and supernatural boldness that you receive in God's presence that changes you.

You leave His presence fortified, restful and full of peace, knowing that there is nothing that God in you cannot handle. You leave His face with divine instructions that will permanently alter the landscape of your life in a positive manner. You can be relieved by having things through fasting and prayers but your true transformation that places you in command of things comes by seeking the face of God. Jesus fasted throughout his earthly ministry not because of any material need in His life. He sought God with an intensity of focus and passion. No wonder He was always in control of situation. He always knew what was to be done under any circumstances.

SEEK THE GOOD OF OTHERS

This is the kind of fasting I want: Free those who are wrongly imprisoned; lighten the burden of those who work for you. Let the oppressed go free and remove the chains that bind people. Share your food with the hungry, and give shelter to the homeless. Give clothes to those who need them, and do not hide from relatives who need your help. Then shall your light break forth..... Isaiah 58:7 (NLT)

Self-centeredness is a product of the flesh. Fasting should be intentionally designed to starve your flesh and destroy its hold on you. As you develop a passionate heart towards God, you need to also develop a compassionate heart towards men. This helps you in ministering to their needs. It becomes a lifestyle and is not to be seen as a form of charity and religious duties that you struggle with.

And if thou draw out thy soul to the hungry, and satisfy the afflicted soul: then shall thy light rise in obscurity, and thy darkness be as the noonday. Isaiah 58:10

As you minister to the needs of others, there is an increase of the deposit of grace in your life for the pursuit of your destiny. It is more blessed to give than to receive. Acts 20:35. Be sensitive to others around you and make yourself available to the Holy Spirit, so He can use you in ministering to their needs. Anytime you minister to the need of others, you minister to God.

> *He that hath pity upon the poor lends unto the Lord; and that which he has given will he pay him again. Proverbs 19:17*

> *Knowing that whatsoever good thing any man doeth, the same shall he receive of the lord whether be he bond or free. Ephesians 6:8*

It is an unfailing principle that the easiest way to connect with the supernatural ladder of progress is seeking God first, others second and yourself last. I know this is not popular with today's mindset. Even among the so-called Charismatic, we have gradually allowed the god of "me first" to have a grip on our soul. I pray that you will shake this python from your life and gain an eternal perspective. Biblical fasting and lifestyle turns attention away from self unto God.

Chapter Four

THE REWARDS OF FASTING

CHAPTER FOUR

THE REWARDS OF FASTING
(What happens when you fast)

Biblical fasting has tremendous rewards.

That thou appear not unto men to fast, but unto thy Father which is in secret: and thy Father, which sees in secret, shall reward thee openly. Matthew 6:18

1. You are spiritually empowered

Fasting is a divine exercise that guarantees your triumph in the race of life.

> *And Jesus returned in the power of the Spirit into Galilee: and there went out a fame of him through the entire region round about. Luke 4:14*

The Holy Spirit led Jesus into the wilderness for a time of fasting and He returned a totally transformed person. The entire landscape of his life, ministry and future was transformed. He came back in the dimension of power that commands the attention of everyone. He commanded the undeniable attention of even his critics and enemy. Every empowerment in the scripture came from the platform of fasting and prayers. Immediately following Jesus' 40 days of fasting in the wilderness, there were several manifestations of God's power and glory in His life and ministry.

> *And Jesus returned in the power of the Spirit into Galilee. Luke 4:14*

His word was with power and men were astonished.

> *And they were astonished at his doctrine; for his word was with power. Luke 4:32*

The powers of darkness recognized the dimension of power on him and they bowed at his appearance.

> *And in the synagogue there was a man, which had a spirit of an unclean devil, and cried out with a loud voice, saying, let us alone: what have we to do with thee, thou Jesus of Nazareth? Art thou come to destroy us? I know thee who thou art: the Holy One of God. Luke 4:33-34*

Are you being terrorized by the powers of darkness? The hour has come that you terminate all of hell's attack on your life through the covenant grace of fasting. Through fasting you can arrest the arrester and destroy the power of the destroyer. Prior to our savior's fasting, there was no record of any manifestation of supernatural power in His ministry. However, he returned, commanding supernatural authority, casting out devils, healing all those who were sick and bringing joy and gladness to the lives of many.

> *And he arose out of the synagogue, and entered into Simon's house. And Simon's wife's mother was taken with a great fever; and they besought him for her. And he stood over her and rebuked the fever and it left her and immediately she arose and ministered unto them. And when the sun was setting, all they that had any sick with divers diseases brought them unto him and he laid his hands on every one of them and healed them. Luke 4:38-40.*

You will experience the manifestation of God's power and glory in your life when there is a thirst and longing in your soul for his presence. There must be a longing through fasting and prayer.

> *O God, thou art my God: early will I seek thee: in a dry and thirsty land, where no water is; to see thy power and thy glory, so as I have seen thee in the sanctuary. Psalms 63:1-2*

2. Fasting transfers your battles to God

> *It came to pass after this also that the children of Moab and the children of Ammon and with other beside the Ammonites came against Jehoshaphat to battle. And Jehoshaphat feared, and set himself to*

seek the Lord and proclaimed a fast throughout all Judah. 2nd Chronicles 20:1,3

King Jehoshaphat's enemies outnumbered him, but he turned to the Lord in fasting and prayer. He committed the raging assault of his enemies to the Lord by proclaiming a fast. God responded to this act of seeking and delivered him and the nation from their enemies.

Ye shall not need to fight in this battle; set yourselves stand ye still and see the salvation of the Lord with you. O Judah and Jerusalem: fear not, nor be dismayed: tomorrow go out against them: for the Lord will be with you. 2nd Chronicles 20:17

If you have ever been confronted with a situation that is seemingly greater than you, the easiest way to victory is transferring the battle to the Lord. Whenever you engage in a fast when faced with any challenge, you are telling God that you are not depending upon your human ability but you are absolutely dependent on Him for victory and deliverance. My wife and I have encountered several challenges in ministry and we prevailed in every case through the intervention of God. This is simply because we have learnt to hand them over to God by faith in fasting and prayer. If God did it before, you can be sure that He will do it again. God did it before as seen in this scripture:

> *Go gather together all the Jews that are present in Shushan, and fast ye for me, and neither eat nor drink three days, night or day: I also and my maidens will fast likewise: and so will I go in unto the King which is not according to the law and if I perish, I perish. Esther 4:16*

The forces of the enemy rose against the Jews in Shushan to totally destroy and eliminate them from the land. Queen Esther rose up with the entire nation to proclaim a fast to the living God. God took over the battle, reversed the satanic verdict, liberated his people and elevated them. What was meant for their destruction became a stepping-stone for their lifting. However this was possible because the people turned their battles to God in fasting. God is a respecter of principles and not of people. What He did for King Jehoshaphat and Queen Esther, He will do for you if you follow this same principle. Irrespective of the battles of life confronting you, I admonish you to cultivate a lifestyle of rolling them to God by faith through fasting. Instead of being fearful and panicking, looking for help from unreliable human sources, humbly place the battle into the unfailing hands of God.

3. Biblical fast grants you access to unusual realm of supernatural revelation

Then shall thy light break forth as the morning.. Isaiah 58:8

There can be no meaningful progress and fruitfulness in a life where darkness rules. Many people toil continually in life without any progress either in their business or in their ministry. The god of this world who is the king and the overseer of the realm of darkness has blinded them with ignorance and lack of foresight. Fasting and prayers breaks the satanic barriers over a life for the shining forth of God's light in the form of revelation wisdom and direction. Whenever a person sees right he can act right to achieve outstanding result.

> *Moreover the word of the Lord came unto me, saying Jeremiah what do you see? And I said, I see a rod of an almond tree. Then said the Lord unto me, thou hast well seen: for I will hasten my word to perform it. Jeremiah 1:11-12*

God's word became effective in Jeremiah's ministry when he saw and embraced the plan and purpose of God for his time. That principle still holds today; the way you see affects the workings of God's word in your life. Gaining a clearer understanding of God's plans and purposes over an issue is the foundation for easy and greater manifestation.

Fasting makes your spirit alert and sensitive to the things of the supernatural. The eye of your spirit is flooded with the light of divine revelation and the ears of your spirit are attuned to heaven's frequency to hear God clearly. The time of fast is the time of seeing things you have never seen before. It is not just a time of prayer but also a time to seek light from heaven. It is a time to seek divine revelation and guidance. Nothing empowers the destiny of a person like divine insight. One word from God can set the pace and change the course of your destiny permanently, for good. The time of fast is usually when you gain fresh understanding of God's word. Portions of the scriptures you have read before will come alive with new revelation during fasting. However, it is not just enough to fast and abstain from food; you need to crave for supernatural insight and supernatural instruction. Spend time in the word of God and the Holy Spirit will grant you access into the mind of God concerning your destiny and the particular situation. He will give you instruction that will result in your elevation because your elevation and promotion are hidden inside the instructions you receive.

And the Lord will guide thee continually...
Isaiah 58:11

4. Fasting is a bondage breaker

He that the Son hath set free is free indeed.
John 8:36

There are various forms of bondages that keeps people bound and does not allow them to enjoy the abundant life that God in Christ has made available for them. Some are under satanic oppression while some are controlled by destructive compulsive addictions to things and substances. Fasting coupled with fervent prayers in the name of Jesus Christ is one of the keys to regaining your total freedom from such compulsive addiction and the oppression of the devil.

> *Shall the prey be taken from the mighty, or the lawful captives delivered? But thus says the Lord, even the captives of the mighty shall be taken away and the prey of the terrible shall be delivered: for I will contend with him that contends with thee and I will save thy children. Isaiah 49:24-25*

Irrespective of the degree of demonic oppression in anybody's life, there is power in the name of Jesus for total liberty. God wants His children to be free indeed. He wants us to enjoy a life of perpetual breakthrough. I have been used of God tremendously in conducting series of deliverance sessions for people and I have witnessed their liberation from various kinds of demonic oppression. I usually see a trend of quick and easy results whenever the person to be delivered is placed on a fasting regimen. Although it is by faith in the authority of Jesus' name and His shed blood that forms the foundation for any form of deliverance, the spiritual condition of the person is also important. I have also seen people who were set free from addictive behaviors or satanic oppression that returned to such behaviors. Jesus warned in his gospel of Luke 11: 24-26 that whenever a person is delivered from demonic occupation of his life, in order to prevent the enemy from coming back with seven more wicked spirits, he must be empowered against re-occupation. Therefore, taking personal responsibility for your deliverance is very vital to staying delivered.

Engaging in the grace of fasting and prayer coupled with the word of God will eliminate the hold of the enemy and that of the flesh in your life. Satan capitalizes on human weakness in the flesh to perpetuate his oppression. Fasting allows your spirit to gain absolute control of your body bringing it under subjection. You will no longer live your life by the dictates and the cravings of the flesh. The flesh is denied of its cravings and carnal desires. Instead of carnal cravings and desires, you will begin to crave for more of the things of the Spirit of God; you will crave for intimacy with God in fellowship through prayer and the word. Subduing your flesh through fasting will make you less vulnerable to any deception brought by the devil.

5. Biblical fast guarantees supernatural health

And your health shall spring forth speedily..
Isaiah 58:8

Many are not living victorious in their health because of excessive eating of hormonally grown foods. It is medically proven that fasting is good for your health. The human body craves for food continually but the irony of life is that eating too much can adversely affect the body. Fasting has both natural and spiritual benefits. It has the natural effect of detoxifying the body to rid it of toxins. In his book "Get Healthy through Detox. and Fasting," Dr. Don Colbert, a medical practitioner, enumerated several medical benefits of living a fasted life such as boosting of the immune system, increased energy, mental clarity, and restorative rest to the digestive tract. Many people are of the opinion that fasting kills! They are under the illusion that they cannot live without food for a while. The biblical truth is that lack of a fasted life is a killer. Eating too much food especially in this day and age of chemically processed foods is the surest way to shorten your life. You are not to live to eat but rather eat to live. *"Man shall not live by bread alone, but by every word that proceeds out of God's mouth." Matthew 4:4*. There is an unexplainable vitality that flows through your entire body during an adventure in fasting. It keeps you vibrant, mentally healthy and spiritually alert in a depressed world.

6. Biblical fast positions you for supernatural supplies

And the Lord shall guide thee continually, and satisfy thy soul in drought, and make fat thy bones: and thou shall be like watered garden, and like spring of water, whose waters fail not.
Isaiah 58:11

A destiny that connects with and ministers to God continually in fasting can never experience dryness in any area of life. Your spirit is always nourished with divine empowerment and you will never be dry in wisdom or understanding. Whenever the flesh or the devil governs a life, such life is subject to depletion. Biblical and acceptable fast keeps the heaven open over a destiny for the continuous supply of God into such life. Prior to the year 1999, things were generally difficult for my wife and me. We lived like we were walking against friction. Tired of this lifestyle, we embarked on 40 days of fasting and prayer. During this period of fasting, we fervently and desperately prayed for a change of status, shattering every satanic hold from our destiny.

In the early hours of March 7, 1999, during one of the fasting series, God visited us in our living room. That visitation in response to our cry changed the landscape of our destinies and that of multitudes. We gained victory over tension, lack, and the forces of limitation. We were not only blessed, we became conduits of blessings to people and nations. By engaging the grace of fasting, we were able to access God's manifest presence that has come to be the hallmark of our lives and ministry. In November of 1999, shortly after the onset of our church ministry, I was led by the Holy Spirit to lead the entire church in a week of fasting and prayer. We met every evening on the church premises praying specifically for various aspects of the ministry. I had a revelation on the first night of the fast. In that revelation, God showed me an orange tree plantation. The ripe fruits had fallen to the ground with little or no human effort. The Spirit of the Lord ministered to me that the church has contacted grace to do ministry with ease and without tears. I was assured in the revelation that just like the orange trees were ripe with fruits, our church ministry would experience unprecedented harvest of souls. This came as a result of the corporate fasting and prayer. The Spirit of the Lord instructed me to continue this exercise by leading the entire church in one week of fasting at the beginning of each month.

Looking back ten years, we thank God for His faithfulness to us in the ministry. Abundant Life Christian Center commission has never lacked in any way. We continue to experience and enjoy supernatural flow of provisions. When our church was three years old, God gave us a building to purchase in the heart of New York City! On the day we closed the deal on the property with the bank and the previous owner, the church made a payment of over four hundred thousand U.S. dollars - in cash! Imagine a three-year old ministry with such amount of savings! Why? Because we broke through the atmosphere of evil that normally suppresses the provisions of ministries and ministers of God. To God be the glory!

We have never and will never experience dryness in membership. To the glory of God, the commission continues to grow in leaps and bounds. You can break through the limit the enemy has placed over your life, family and ministry if you will engage in this glorious adventure today. This *"kind"* goes out not but by fasting and prayer. Matthew 17:21. Jesus instructed us here that some challenges will be overcome easily but some require consistent and persistent fasting and prayer for total breakthrough. Don't settle for the lie of the enemy that you are meant to live a barren and dry life. Jesus came to usher you into the family of those enjoying the abundant life in Him. I challenge you to rise up today and embrace this adventure as part of your daily walk, without being dogmatic about it, but as a living force of the Christ life.

Chapter Five

FASTING, A DIVINE BOOSTER IN KNOWING THE WILL OF GOD

CHAPTER FIVE

FASTING, A DIVINE BOOSTER IN KNOWING THE WILL OF GOD. (How To Know The Will of God)

Knowing the will of God or how to be led by the spirit of God in decision-making is one of the keys to your breakthrough. Fasting is a booster in the school of divine direction. Fasting releases the spirit of men from all junk and things that clog the spirit. This will enable us to freely receive from God. The cheapest way to terminate frustration in life and to avoid living a life of collective mistakes is to be able to hear from God. However, most Christians have difficulties in this area. They have made it sound like a religious and uphill task. From this moment, I want you to greatly desire this great spiritual adventure that will alter the landscape of your destiny permanently for good. It will add color and beauty to your name. Knowing how to be led by God has been a great source of strength in my Christian journey. It is helping me to soar high where others are groping in the dark.

I will instruct thee and teach thee in the way which thou shall go. I will guide thee with mine

> *eye. Be ye not as the horse, or as the mule, which have no understanding: whose mouth must be held in with a bit and bridle, lest they come near unto thee. Psalms 32:8-9*

It is so interesting to know that God is eager to provide clear guidance for His children and that includes you and me. He does not want us to be like mules being dragged about by circumstances, or by human and satanic manipulations. As a New Testament believer, you can and should expect to be led by the Spirit of God.

There are several benefits to being led by the Sprit of the living God. Here are just two examples:

1. It terminates frustrations and brings clarity to the present and the future.

There is an innate desire in every human, wanting to know what to do and how to do it. The revealed Word of God is the clear mandate and the will of God for his children. We are to live our lives satisfied by the word of God and not based upon any vision. There are Christians who are constantly depending on daily visions or the spectacular, before making day-to-day decisions. We are to walk by faith, depending on the word of God to guide us. His word is a lamp to your feet, and a light unto your path (Psalm 119:105). However, there are times we need specific directions on particular issues of our lives that are not clearly spelt out by the scripture. Examples of such decisions include who to marry, whether to relocate to a particular place or not, the types of business to embark upon, etc. Since you cannot afford to play the game of luck with major life issues, it becomes necessary to seek the mind of God. Knowing His mind and His specific will on any issue will terminate any frustration caused by consequences of wrong choices.

> *And David enquired at the Lord saying, Shall I pursue after this troop? Shall I overtake them? And he answered him, pursue: for thou shall surely overtake them, and without fail recover all.*
> 1 Samuel 30:8

In the encounter above, David and six hundred of his men lost all their possessions to their enemies. Their houses were burnt down; the enemies took their wives and children away as captives. This brought panic, confusion and frustration into the lives of these men. They wept until they had no more strength to weep. David engaged God in knowing what to do. He received specific direction and recovered all. I prophetically believe that this is your season for the total recovery of all you have lost in life. Fasting breaks the yoke and the grip of the enemy over your inheritance. It sharpens your spirit man to be sensitive and alert to the things of God. Whatever you have lost or whatever the enemy has stolen from you, the bridge to total restoration is engaging in this adventure of fasting coupled with divine direction.

2. It keeps you above human or demonic manipulation.

For all that God has for you, Satan also has counterfeits. Many people have fallen victims to the manipulations of men in an attempt to know the will of God for their lives. People seek direction and guidance through various mediums not approved by God such as palm readers, stargazers, tarot cards and horoscopes. These are satanic and human mediums that are not approved by God. They may accurately predict certain events in your past using familiar spirits; however, it is satanic and will ultimately keep you in human bondage. The Spirit of the Lord once ministered to me that whenever I allow God to lead me, I can not be misled by men. And whenever I allow the Spirit of God to lead me, men cannot leave me behind.

HOW CAN I BE LED?

God enlightens and guides us through various means such as: Inward witness of His Spirit, Inward voice of His Spirit, through His word, through dreams and visions, through circumstances and through prophetic vessels.

One of the surest and safest ways God leads us is through the inward witness of His Spirit inside of us. Being led by God doesn't have to be in a spectacular manner.

> *The Spirit itself bears witness with our spirit, that we are the children of God.* Romans 8:16
>
> *The spirit of man is the candle of the Lord, searching all the inward parts of the belly.* Proverbs 20:27

Man is a tripartite being. Man is first a spirit, housed in a human body and having a soul. Feeling is the voice of the body. Reasoning is the voice of the soul and the conscience is the voice of the spirit. Since God is Spirit, He communicates with us through our spirit man. The above scripture in Proverbs 20:27 in another translation says, *"The spirit of man is the lamp of the Lord."* What it means is that God will enlighten and guide us through our spirits. It can come as an inner gentle whisper of the Holy Spirit or as what some call intuition or a hunch or a nudge. Since you have been born again by the Spirit of the living God, you can be rest assured that He will lead you on specific issues by releasing an inner witness that settles on your spirit man. Whether you call it an intuition, a hunch or a nudge, you need to believe by faith that it is God speaking to you. And as you develop your spirit man and your relationship with God, you will learn to trust God and rely on Him more to speak to you in this manner. This comes easily when you learn to train your spirit by consistently feeding it with God's word, communicating with God in prayer, and living in obedience to God's word.

> *But as it is written, eye has not seen, nor ear heard, neither have entered into the heart of man, the things which God has prepared for them that love him. But God has revealed them unto us by his Spirit: for the Spirit searches all things, yea the deep things of God. For what man knows the things of a man except the spirit of man which is in him? Even so the things of God knows no man but the Spirit of God. Now we have received not the spirit of the world but the Spirit, which is of God: that we might know the things that are freely given to us of God. 1st Corinthians 2:9-12*

My wife and I were driving from Brooklyn, New York to the Bronx, also in New York City in November of 1999. We had another Sister traveling with us inside the car. Shortly after saying a prayer, we were all in a cordial discussion when suddenly I had an inner nudge to start praying in the spirit. My wife and the sister sensed my sudden shift and they also joined me in the prayer. While we were still praying we heard a sudden bang and a loud noise and we realized that a gun bullet had struck the windshield of our vehicle. The windshield which was not a bulletproof shield held the bullet and did not allow it to kill any of us. A non-bullet proof windshield is not designed to stop gun bullets. The supernatural hands of God stopped the bullet in response to our prayers. We escaped death by following the leadings of God through an inner nudge. Blessed be God for evermore! You do not have to see a bright light from heaven, neither do you have to hear a very loud baritone voice from the sky; God can speak to you in an audible voice but that is not always the usual way. Apostle Paul had received an instruction through an impression to his spirit in the book of Acts during his voyage to Rome. It was this encounter that saved the lives of about 277 men inside the boat.

> *And Paul said unto them, Sirs, I perceive that this voyage will be with hurt and much damage, not only of the lading and ship but also of our lives.*
> *Acts 27:10*

Paul perceived and sensed the imminent danger inside of his spirit. Thank God for Paul's spiritual intervention through fasting; this led to the preservation of their lives, even though they had rejected his counsel.

> *But after long fasting, Paul stood forth in the midst of them and said, Sirs, you should have hearkened unto me and not have sailed from Crete, and to have gained this harm and loss and now I exhort you to be of good cheer: for there shall be no loss of any man's life among you but of the ship. For there stood by me this night the angel of God whose I am and whom I serve, saying fear not Paul: thou must be brought before Caesar, and lo God has given thee all that sail with thee.*
> *Acts 27:21-24*

What a glorious doorway God has opened for us through the grace of fasting in order for us to shatter the wickedness of the wicked and be able to reverse the seemingly irreversible situations of life. Apostle Paul received this crucial revelation from God by perceiving it inside of his spirit.

Another major way by which God can lead us is through His Word. God has a solution for anything you encounter in life, in His Word. Whenever you engage in the study of the written Word of God, He, by His Spirit quickens you to receive instructions from Him. For example in November of 2009, I was fasting and praying, asking God for the theme of the month for our commission. In one of my daily devotions, while studying and meditating on the epistle of 1st Peter 1:3, the Holy Spirit quickened my spirit and gave me a revelation on this phrase, "the supernatural power of a living hope." God downloaded into my spirit several ministrations and teachings for the entire month from this one verse of the scripture. The power of God was released in a greater proportion throughout our churches and many testimonies of changed lives and situations abounded to the glory of His name. I had read that same portion of scripture many times in the past without such revelation. This is what is called "Rhema;" when the written word becomes a living word inside of you. The frequency of such revelation is higher during fasting because you are more spiritually sensitive and alert to the things of God.

The Holy Spirit is also given to guide us into knowing the will of God. The Voice of the Spirit is a sure way by which God leads His people.

> *Howbeit when the Spirit of truth is come, he will guide you into all truth: for he shall not speak of himself; but whatsoever he shall hear, that shall he speak; and HE WILL SHOW YOU THINGS TO COME. He shall glorify me: for HE SAHALL RECEIVE OF MINE AND SHALL SHEW IT UNTO YOU. John 16:13-14*

The Holy Spirit of God that lives inside every believer is given to guide us. He will tell us what to do and what not to do. We are more attuned to hearing from Him also during fasting.

> *Then the Spirit said unto Phillip, go near and join yourself to this chariot. Acts 8:29.*

As you cultivate the art of listening to the Holy Spirit inside of you, He connects you with the signal of heaven for divine leading.

Some people find it difficult to receive directly from God because they think that God will always speak to them in a spectacular manner such as hearing an audible voice from heaven, or through the appearance of an angel. Even though God can and still speaks to us through an audible voice or through his angels, we should expect

Him to speak to us in anyway He chooses and not in a particular way.

God can also lead us through dreams, through prophetic insight from genuine human vessels ordained of God or by listening to Holy Spirit-inspired teachings from such human vessels. He can lead us through circumstances. Satan can also counterfeit any of these methods in an attempt to bring confusion to a destiny. You must therefore always pray for the grace to discern. The safest guide from falling into the error of the enemy is by subjecting whatever revelation you receive to the word of God. Some have asked questions on how to differentiate between the voice of their human spirit and that of the Spirit of God or how to ascertain if a dream or any message is of God.

> *For the word of God is quick, and powerful, and sharper than any two edged sword, piercing even to the dividing asunder of soul and spirit and of the joints and marrow and it is a discerner of the thoughts and intents of the heart. Hebrews 4:12.*

You simply subject it to the word of God because God will never instruct you contrary to His word. Satan will never also instruct you to obey the word of God. He will always lead you contrary to God's word. He may suggest something similar but it will be done in such a manner that will not bring glory to God's name.

I must always warn that prophetic messages given to you by a human vessel must be confirmational rather than instructional. It is usually meant to be a confirmation of what is already being dealt to you or spoken to you by the Spirit of God. Be very careful on making the major decisions of your life based on messages given to you by human vessels because it is greatly subject to error. Pray over it again and again and seek confirmation from God. In all these cases however, fasting makes it a lot easier to receive from God because it unclogs our spiritual senses from natural and spiritual hindrances.

Chapter Six

THE ROLE OF PRAYER IN FASTING

CHAPTER SIX

THE ROLE OF PRAYER IN FASTING:
(The Prayer Connection)

Howbeit, this kind goes out but by prayer and fasting. Matthew 17:21

In my book, "Pathways to Breakthrough," I wrote that "fasting and prayer go together." Fasting without prayer is a hunger strike. Fasting without prayer is like a car without wheels. You will only make noise, but you are not going anywhere. Fasting is the brother of prayer that keeps the spirit in tune and enables the person to seek God's face with greater intensity of purpose.

During your time of fast it is very important that you set sufficient time apart to pray. It is not abstaining from food in itself that gives you the desired result and breakthrough; it is engaging in fervent prayer during the period of fasting that does. You may have to drag yourself to the altar of prayer but there is a grace that is released as you begin to pray. Fasting is a prayer booster. There is a dimension of focus and energy that is released into your prayer life as a result of a fasted lifestyle. You become more spiritually sensitive, alert and burdened to pray. Virtually everywhere fasting is mentioned in both the Old and the New Testaments, it is usually coupled with prayer.

> *So we fasted and besought our God for this and He heard our entreaty. Ezra 8:23*
>
> *And when they ministered to the Lord and fasted the Holy Ghost said, "separate me Barnabas and Saul for the work whereunto I have called them." And when they had fasted and prayed and laid their hands on them they sent them away. Acts 13:2-3*

Whenever prayer is accompanied with fasting, it generates maximum and immediate results from the throne room of grace. Prayer is communicating with God on the platform of our covenant relationship of the shed blood of Jesus Christ. It is stepping boldly to the throne of grace to receive strength and locate divine help for the journey of life. Prayer is the altar where we literally deliver our destinies and circumstances to God. It is also an avenue to engage the power of God in gaining absolute victory over the works of darkness in your life. It is still the divine avenue by which destinies can be transformed and liberated from the oppression of darkness. Are you challenged at this hour to the point of almost quitting? I say to you in the words of Jesus Christ and by the grace of God granted me as an agent of change; don't quit! Discouragement is a thief and a robber of destiny. Jesus said men ought always to pray and not to faint. Luke

THE ROLE OF PRAYER IN FASTING

18:1. I challenge you to engage yourself once again in this glorious adventure that has lifted many from the pit of affliction to the throne of dominion. Daniel, through consistent prayer and fasting coupled with a Godly lifestyle became a trans-generational leader in an ungodly Babylonian empire. With it he subdued Kingdoms and shut the mouths of lions. Rise up child of God and take your place of dominion through fasting and prayer.

CONDITIONS FOR PRAYERS TO BE ANSWERED

a) You must be a child of God which means you must have a daily living relationship with God through the atonement work of Jesus Christ on the cross of Calvary. Matthew 6:9, John 1:12, John 3:3-4

b) You must pray IN FAITH unto THE FATHER through the NAME OF JESUS CHRIST. Matthew 11:22-24, Mark 2-5, Matthew 6:9, John 16:23, John 13:23-24, Luke 10:19

c) Your prayers must be based on the Word of God. Ezekiel 12:28, Psalm 138:2, Psalm 89:4

d) There must not be any root of un-forgiveness, bitterness or anger in you. Make sure you forgive and release those who sinned against you. (This is a must!)

AN INSATIABLE HUNGER

In my Christian journey I have realized one major key that separates the winners from the losers. It is the key that distinguishes the victorious from the depressed. It is the key that demarcates those who live to please God from those who don't. That vital key is developing an insatiable hunger for more of God irrespective of your level of achievement. The key is to be a God-chaser and not a God-user.

> *Another parable put he forth unto them saying: The kingdom of heaven is likened unto a man who sowed good seed in his field. But while men slept, his enemy came and sowed tares among the wheat, and went his way. Matthew 13:24-25*

The man in the parable above allowed the enemy to encroach on his destiny because he lost the hunger and the zeal for God and the things of God. He was in deep spiritual slumber. Spiritual slumber is usually as a result of lack of spiritual hunger and thirst for God and the things of God. Many have allowed little success or life challenges to kill their hunger for God. In today's Christianity, the church of God is not in short supply of revelations. The Christians today have access to spiritual materials more than any past generations, but the church today, lacks the power of God. This is as a result of a lack of zeal for God's presence in fasting and prayer. Many are just satisfied to be on the same spiritual plane from day to day.

THE ROLE OF PRAYER IN FASTING

> *As the deer pants after the water brooks so pants my soul after thee. O God. My soul thirsts for God for the living God: when shall I come and appear before God? My tears have been my meat day and night, while they continually say unto me, where is thy God? Psalm 42:1-3*

One of the secrets responsible for my progress in life and ministry is the desire to always seek the face of God. When was the last time you embarked on fasting not for things but as a form of worship to access the presence of God? There must be a burning desire inside of you to know God better in your daily walk. When you hunger for God, He will fill you with His glory. It is dangerous to live on the same spiritual plane for too long; you must always refill your spiritual tank. Living a fasted lifestyle is the antidote to spiritual barrenness and dryness. You don't wait until there is a problem before you embark on fasting; it should be part of your fruitful Christian adventure on the earth.

> *In the last day, that great day of the feast, Jesus stood and cried saying, If any man thirst, let him come unto me, and drink. He that believes on me, as the scripture has said, out of his belly shall flow rivers of living water. John 7:37-38.*

Jesus gave us an insight to enjoying a fruitful life in the kingdom. He says *"If any man thirst let him come and drink..."* When you drink of the supernatural flow of grace from heaven, you become an unending source of power, joy, and exploits. Every Christian should endeavor to set apart certain days in the week for fasting. Never arrive at a point in your walk with God that you lose the hunger and thirst for His presence. Since giving my life to Christ over 20 years ago, I have been consistent in devoting certain days of the week in seeking God, not for material things, but for more of Him. In August 1999, my wife and I did a forty day fast with just one prayer request from Luke 24:49; *"that God should endue us with His power from on high for kingdom assignment."* We were not pastors then but church workers. God honored our request and baptized us with "The Breakthrough Anointing" for the liberation of multitudes in our generation and generations to come. Ten years later, despite his countless blessings in our lives and ministries, we are still passionate seekers of His presence in fasting and prayer. You may be genuinely called by God to do whatever you are doing but you must be willing to pay the price for the call.

Chapter Seven

DAILY PRAYER GUIDE FOR MORNING DEVOTION

CHAPTER SEVEN

DAILY PRAYER GUIDE FOR MORNING DEVOTION

Psalm 100:1-5; Lamentation 3:22-23; Psalm 5:3; Mark 1:35; Romans 8:26

Those who look up to him will be radiant with joy, no shadow of shame will darken their faces. Psalm 34:5. The way each day will look to you begins with whom you behold daily. See the face of God before you see the face of men.

Note:

This is not a catechism or a religious formula. It is to serve as a guide and not a guard.

Do not be too rigid and mechanical in praying these prayer points. Give the Holy Spirit the freedom in leading you. You can pray each prayer item many times before moving to the next as the Holy Spirit leads you.

Begin your day singing praises unto the Lord. Being alive is not your right but a privilege.

Enter into his presence with thanksgiving, and with praise. Be thankful unto him and bless his name. For his goodness and mercy that is keeping you daily. [Sing any praise or worship song that the Holy Spirit brings into your mind. Sing also in the spirit (tongue)].

Declare that the Lord is God, that He is the one who has made you and that you are His child, the apple of His eyes. Declare that this is the day the Lord has made and that you will rejoice and be glad in it.

Romans 8:26 The Holy Spirit is your indwelling prayer partner at the beginning of every prayer time; invite Him to energize, empower, and strengthen you as follows:

> *"I now by faith commit my prayer time into the hand of the Holy Spirit; I hereby yield my WILL, my INTELLECT, my MIND, my EMOTIONS and my VOCAL CORD to the Holy Spirit. I thank you Holy Spirit for helping me to pray the will of God concerning my life effectively and diligently."*

Rebuke any form of distraction; rebuke early morning heaviness, confusion, worry, depression or any hangover resulting from bad dreams. Cancel any spirit of procrastination that may want you to postpone this prayer time.

Heavenly father, immerse me in your mercy. Forgive me of any forms of sin in my life. Cleanse me with the blood of Jesus as I have forgiven others of their sins. I forgive and release right now all that have hurt or sinned

THE ROLE OF PRAYER IN FASTING

against me. I flush bitterness out of my heart in any form in Jesus name.

Pray Lamentation 3:22-23 and pray in the Holy Ghost as led. Charge your spirit with the mercy of God. Pray that you have been established by His mercy. Pray that you will be preserved and protected today and not consumed because of His mercy.

PRAY THE FOLLOWING PRAYERS:

By the blood of Jesus, I declare that my mind is alert. I declare that my spiritual eyes are opened to see the way God wants me to see. I will see possibilities and opportunities that heaven has apportioned for me today. I refuse to bow to the forces of excuses and failure today.

In the name of Jesus, I seek wisdom that is from above. I will increase in Godly wisdom, prudence and wise judgment.

By the authority in the name of Jesus, I silence all demonic accusers rising up against my destiny, ministry, career and family today in Jesus name. This is my day of goodness, restoration and joy.

By the authority in the name of Jesus, I declare today as the day of manifestation of my glory. Heavenly father, let everything covering the manifestation of my glory be removed in Jesus name.

Heavenly father, in accordance to your word, I decree that the devices of the wicked concerning my family and me be disappointed in Jesus name. I cancel every bad news, losses or evil concerning today, which has been programmed last night by evil powers in Jesus name.

I decree good news upon my destiny today as I go out. I decree restoration, grace, courage, boldness, riches, favor, honor, joy and peace concerning my destiny today in Jesus name.

I decree in the name of Jesus that God will overwhelm me with the unction for supernatural increase. God will cause me to break forth on the right hand and on the left: (I will increase in every area of my life: spiritual, finance, wisdom, coordinated insight in Jesus name.) Isaiah 54:2-3

By the authority in the name of Jesus, I decree that every wall of containment holding me back from experiencing my God's given increase should crumble in Jesus name!

Heavenly father let your lifting hand rest strongly upon my life and bring forth a divine lifting today and henceforth in Jesus name. Psalm 75:6. May you enlarge my coast, extend my capacity and make me a person of influence and affluence in Jesus name. 1st Chronicles 4:9-10

By the authority in the name of Jesus, I pray that the Lord will open my eyes of understanding today and grant

THE ROLE OF PRAYER IN FASTING

me revelation and knowledge to know the very strategies that will bring supernatural increase into my destiny. Ephesians 1:17-19.

I rebuke the spirit of waste, procrastination, laziness, slothfulness, slumber and dullness of heart from my life today and forevermore in Jesus name. I receive a sound mind for increase in Jesus name.

By the authority in the name of Jesus, I receive today the grace to walk worthy of my calling as a child of God in all manner of holiness and purity.

I receive the grace and unction to be a kingdom-minded Christian, with passion to please God in all my ways.

I declare today that I will not live for self but for the cause of the gospel of Jesus Christ. Make me a blessing to others today.

I pray for all believers, ministers of the gospel and I ask that you uphold them from evil today in Jesus name. (Pray for your Pastor and family now)

Pray for the salvation of loved ones/sinners in general. Lord use me to win souls as I go out today. I claim the salvation of the following people....(mention their names)

As I go out today, let me encounter helpers of destiny who will go out of their way to help me in Jesus name. Lord, baptize me with fresh favor in Jesus name.

Pray that God should endue you with His power so that you can reach out to the lost, pray fervently, read His word with understanding, etc. Luke 24:49

Pray that all the strategies, plans, schemes and the plot of the wicked ones concerning you be exposed and destroyed in Jesus name. Isaiah 54:15-17.

I command and decree that every weapon formed against me in any realm of existence, whether in the air, in the sea, under the sea, etc be cancelled in Jesus name Job 22:28

Pray as you are led now on any issue. PRAY IN THE HOLY GHOST.

Lord grant me the grace to study your Word, to be prayerful and be holy throughout the day.

Pray as you are led again on any issue still bothering you or any specific ministration from the bible that you have read. PRAY IN THE HOLY GHOST AGAIN.

I thank you God for hearing and answering all my prayers today. I thank you also for speaking in your Word to me. Receive all the praise and glory for all you have done and will do today, in Jesus name.

CLOSING PRAYER FOR MORNING SESSION:

"I thank you Holy Spirit, for being my indwelling prayer partner. As I conclude my morning session I thank you that my mind is alert, I am focused on the things from above, and my mind is focused on profitable things. Thank you for sensitizing me and giving me the grace to pray effectively in the afternoon." Or "I thank you for reminding me and giving me the ability to pray effective prayer in the afternoon."

EVENING DEVOTIONAL PLAN

Do not be rigid and mechanical. Commit this prayer hour to the Holy Spirit and ask for His strength, guidance and grace. Romans 8:26. Pray each prayer item many times before moving to the next.

Father, I worship your wonderful name for all you have done for my entire family and me today. I bless your name for your untold deliverances today. I thank you also for provision and protection.

Sing praise and worship songs to bless God and fellowship with Him as you are led now.

Lord, I ask for your forgiveness in any way I have sinned against you today in my words, deeds and actions, I ask that you cleanse me with the blood of Jesus.

Lord, I commit this night into your hands. I ask that you give your angels charge over me and my family to guide and protect us in Jesus name.

Lord, I pray for the restoration of whatever good things I lost today. Restore my joy, anointing, favor, promotion and every good opportunity lost in Jesus name.

I come against every evil dream, every attack of the enemy and nightmares concerning my family and my ministry in Jesus name.

I take authority and dominion over every plan of the witches, wizard and all agents of darkness tonight in Jesus name. None of their weapons fashioned against me shall prosper.

Pray about any painful issue or incident that happened today and is threatening your peace. Put it in God's hand and rest on Him. Receive peace now. Isaiah 26:3

Lay your hands on your head now and begin blessing your entire life. Decree the blessings of the Lord over your life.

My head rejects shame this year and beyond. I choose glory and not shame. I choose to shine. I choose to lend and not borrow. I choose to rejoice and not sorrow. I choose to live and not die in Jesus name.

I cover myself, my family, my relations, and friends, with the blood of Jesus.

I soak this house, all the properties including the entire neighborhood in the blood of Jesus and I forbid the activities of agents of darkness in Jesus name.

THE ROLE OF PRAYER IN FASTING

Lord, build a wall of fire around my life, family, job, academics, business, career and ministry tonight in Jesus name.

Lord, I thank you for causing my spirit to be violent against the spirit of darkness in my sleep and dream.

I ask that you be with me and reveal strategies and wisdom for progress unto me in my dream tonight in Jesus name.

Thank you Lord because you give your beloved sleep. I will sleep peacefully without any nightmare and I will wake up strong and fresh in Jesus name.

I thank you Lord for hearing and answering my prayers in Jesus name.

I thank you Lord for waking me up in the night by the help of the Holy Spirit and thank you for enabling me to pray fervently and to study your word with understanding.

(You may repeat any of these points again now as you are led or you can include other prayer points).

OTHER PRAYER POINTS

PRAYER TO CANCEL EVIL/BAD DREAMS

Heavenly father, I commit my dream life into your hands in Jesus name. I subject everyone, everyplace, situations or things I see in the dream through the blood of Jesus and I nullify their effects on my life and destiny in Jesus name.

I pull down every altar of darkness erected against my life causing me to experience bad dreams in Jesus name.

Let all evil dreams I have had, or other people have had concerning me be cancelled and nullified in Jesus name.

Let all losses in the dream be converted to gains in Jesus name.

Let all weakness in the dream be converted to strength.

Let all evil food I ate in the dream be neutralized by the authority in the name of Jesus.

Let all evil pursuits in the dream be converted to purpose and power in Jesus name.

Let all failures in the dream be converted to fortunes and let all trials in the dream be converted into testimonies in Jesus name.

Let all evil dreams..... (be specific and mention them) be cancelled and nullified now in Jesus name. (Pray until you have peace in your heart that you have prayed through).

I bind and inhibit the operation of every spirit that engages me in sexual relationship in the dream in Jesus name. I disengage from every relationship with such spirit because I am in a covenant relationship with the Lord Jesus.

I receive wisdom and grace for the interpretation of necessary dreams. And I also receive wisdom in making right decisions to avoid the manifestations of bad dreams and also wisdom to enhance the fulfillment of good dreams in Jesus name.

PRAYER FOR PREGNANT WOMEN
Exodus 23:26, Philippians 1:6

Heavenly father, I commit this baby into your unfailing hand. I pray that you keep this baby to full term in Jesus name.

I reject miscarriage and premature birth concerning this pregnancy in Jesus name. I shall not cast my young before the appointed time in Jesus name.

I come against death in pregnancy. I shall experience safe delivery. My baby and I shall not die but live during and after delivery in Jesus name.

Heavenly father, I pray that you will direct all the medical personnel to function well and that there will be no mistake in Jesus name.

Lay your hands on your womb now and prophesy to your baby. Thank God for answered prayers.

PRAYER FOR PHYSICAL HEALING AGAINST SICKNESS AND DISEASE

Exodus 15:26, Deut. 7:15, 1 Peter 2:24, Isaiah 53:1-5

Thank you Jehovah Rapha, You are the Lord who heals me and delivers me from all sicknesses and diseases. I bind every demon of sickness and infirmity in my body in Jesus name. I command every sickness (call it by name if you can) to leave my body now, by the authority in the name of Jesus.

No weapon fashioned against me shall prosper and every tongue that rises against me to afflict me with sickness shall not prosper in Jesus name. Every tongue risen against me in judgment I condemn now in Jesus name.

Every tree my heavenly father has not planted shall be uprooted, I command that everything that Satan and his cohorts have planted in my body be uprooted and destroyed in Jesus name. I boldly declare according to 1st Peter 2:24, that by the stripes of Jesus, I am healed from the crown of my head to the soles of my feet. My body is the temple of the Holy Spirit; and God cannot share His temple with sickness; therefore, I command sickness and disease to vacate my body in Jesus name.

The rod of the wicked cannot rest upon the lot of the righteous, I belong to Jesus, and therefore, I command every satanic rod of wickedness to depart from my body in Jesus name.

I declare today that my entire household and I will continue to enjoy good health in Jesus name.

[PRAY IN THE SPIRIT- PRAY IN TONGUES FOR FEW MINUTES]

PRAYER FOR WISDOM
James 1:5, Proverb 4:7

Father, you said if anyone lacks wisdom, let him ask of You, therefore, I ask in faith today that I will be filled with the knowledge of Your will in all wisdom and spiritual understanding.

Today, I incline my ears to wisdom, and apply my heart to understanding so that I might receive that which has been freely given to me.

In the name of Jesus, I receive skills necessary for my advancement and godly wisdom and instruction.

I acquire divine skills and attain to sound counsels so that I may be able to steer the course of my life rightly.

Father, in the name of Jesus, I look carefully to how I walk! I live purposefully and worthily and accurately, not as unwise and witless, but as a wise, sensible, intelligent person; making the very most of my time - buying up every opportunity. I thank you that I receive divine wisdom to prosper from now and henceforth.

I receive the divine wisdom to acquire and manage my God-given resources spiritually, materially, financially, emotionally, and relationally.

I receive the divine wisdom to be a good ambassador of God's kingdom on earth.

Father I just want to thank you that I have wisdom and knowledge to dream beyond my means.

[PRAY IN THE SPIRIT- PRAY IN TONGUES FOR FEW MINUTES]

PRAYER FOR DIRECTION AND INSTRUCTION (ILLUMINATION)
Ephesians 1:17 & 18. (Amplified)

I thank you God, the father of our Lord Jesus Christ, the Father of glory. I pray that you grant unto me the spirit of wisdom and revelation of insight into mysteries and secrets in the deep and intimate knowledge of you.

Thank you that the eye of my heart is flooded with light, so that I can know and understand the hope of your calling upon my life, and the riches of your glorious inheritance in the saints. I decree that I will henceforth not walk in confusion.

I thank you that my mind and heart are illuminated by the light that flows from you and I will not walk in confusion.

I receive and embrace into my spirit man the divine direction and instruction for the fulfillment of my vision, the prosperity of my business, the manifestation of my promotion, and the enlargement of my coast in Jesus name.

PRAYER FOR KNOWING GOD'S WILL

Psalm 32:8. Proverb 4:18, John 10:3-4, 1 Corinthians 1:30

Father, I thank You that You are instructing me in the way which I should go and that You are guiding me with Your eyes. I thank You for Your guidance and leading concerning Your will, Your plan, and Your purpose for my life. I do hear the voice of the Good Shepherd, for I know You and follow You. You lead me in the path of righteousness for your name sake.

Thank You, Father that my path is growing brighter until it reaches the full light of day. As I follow You, Lord, I believe my path is becoming clearer each day.

Thank You, Father, that Jesus was made wisdom unto me. Confusion is not part of my life. I trust in You and lean not unto my own understanding. As I acknowledge You in all my ways, You are directing my paths. I believe that as I trust in You completely, You will show me the path of life.

PRAYER FOR ABILITY TO PRODUCE WEALTH

Deuteronomy 8:18. But you shall remember the Lord your God, for it is He Who gives you power to get wealth that He may establish His covenant which He swore to your fathers, as it is this day.

Dear heavenly father, I acknowledge you as my God that gives me the ability, the opportunity and the favor to produce wealth.

By faith in Jesus name, I hereby receive the ability to produce wealth.

By faith in Jesus name, I receive and begin to utilize opportunities to produce wealth.

By faith in Jesus name, I receive both human and divine favor to produce wealth

By faith in Jesus name, I receive God given relationships to produce wealth

By faith in Jesus name, I receive the divine endowment to produce wealth

By faith in Jesus name, I receive the divine insight, concept and the ideas for witty inventions and creativity in Jesus name.

[PRAY IN THE SPIRIT- PRAY IN TONGUES FOR FEW MINUTES]

PRACTICAL TIPS DURING FASTING AND PRAYER

- Do not broadcast to the world that you are fasting. Matthew 6:16-18

- Make sure you do not let the drive to eat physical food dominate you. Always pray and ask the Holy Spirit to focus your mind on spiritual food [The Word of God]

- Develop God's consciousness rather than constantly checking your clock. It is profitable to break your fast and have energy to pray and study the word.

- Fasting without prayer and meditation on God's Word is hunger strike with no divine blessing. Matthew 4:4.

- Write down your prayer requests in your prayer journal at the onset of the fast. Look for scriptures to back up each prayer points. Pray on these items day and night and by faith believe that you have the answers.

- Make sure you are sensitive to the inner voice of the Holy Spirit to instruct and guide you in receiving answers to your prayers. Take note of instructions received during this period.

- It is advisable that you endeavor to wake up to pray and meditate on God's Word in the night.

- It is advisable that you drink clear pure water during a prolonged period of fasting.

- Above all, use fasting as a tool to enhance your relationship with God.

- Fasting should make you better in every area of your life especially your character. Read Isaiah chapter 58 daily.

Chapter Eight

PROOFS OF PREVAILING PRAYERS

CHAPTER EIGHT

PROOFS OF PREVAILING PRAYERS

I died but Prayer brought me back to Life!

One day while I was at a choir rehearsal in the church sanctuary, I passed-out and regained consciousness after 48 hours. One of the pastors later narrated to me that people thought that I was in trance until they noticed that I was motionless.

Choir members started praying and Emergency Medical Services (EMS) were called. I was told that before the ambulance came, I was not breathing and I didn't have a pulse.

One of the choir members, who is a medical doctor, was at rehearsal that day and while others were praying, she began to give me mouth-to-mouth resuscitation (CPR).

One of the Doctors at the hospital where I was later taken in order to fulfill the requirement of the law and to fully recover, confirmed that it was a miracle that I was alive. She pointed out that in her years in the medical field, most people that suffered such type of cardiac arrest died as a result or suffer major brain damage. The EMS workers from Brookdale Hospital, Brooklyn New York were also shocked that I was alive, because they tried all but could not bring me back to regain my consciousness.

The Bible says that the prayer of the righteous avails much; the Choir members, the Pastors kept praying and I was anointed with the anointed oil which was always on the altar, until I was brought back to life. I give God all the glory for bringing me to Abundant Life Christian Center where I have received spiritual support and nurturing that planted me on a higher level of faith and established me as a prayer warrior. —Sister H. James

I was going to commit suicide but I am now the CEO of my own company!

I walked into Abundant Life Christian Center (ALCC) on August 27th 2006 and little did I know that I was walking into a life-changing ministry. I came into ALCC hopeless and depressed. My family was by my side, yet I felt so lonely and helpless. I had never met Pastor Festus Adeyeye or even heard of him but thank God who led us to ALCC on that Sunday. I was tired of life; I had no job and no money to feed my family. It was all planned out in my mind that I was going to take my life that faithful Sunday night after service. But on that same day, my wife and I and our children attended church service at ALCC.

Pastor Festus Adeyeye stepped on the pulpit, and the Lord spoke through him, saying, "There is someone here for the first time and you are planning on taking your life because you think all is over for you, but the God I serve says to tell you not to do it; that two weeks from today, 'I the Lord God of Host' will turn around things for you."

Truly two weeks came and my situation turned around for good, and since then life has been good. It has been three years now and a man with no hope, no job, and no money has become the CEO of his own company. God is good; truly God is with Pastor Festus Adeyeye and his wife. —Brother O. John

The 24-Hour Miracle

Exactly 24 hours after the word of knowledge was given on a Sunday morning by Pastor Festus Adeyeye, we received a supernatural miracle from God in fulfillment of the word that was spoken. This is the testimony of the wonderful things God has done for us. This testimony is a demonstration that when the altar of extraordinary praise is lifted up to God, He does extraordinary wonders.

On Saturday, September 12, 2009, I asked the Lord where He would have us go for worship. I felt Him leading us to Abundant Life Christian Center, the home of winners, over-comers and champions, where men and women are prepared to take the nations for Christ. I knew that the Lord had a word for me, but this testimony is not about me. It is about the faithfulness of God's spoken word. He speaks it and it stands. And blessed are those who run with His word.

God changed the life of a young man as a result of the atmosphere of extravagant praise and the pure, unmixed spoken word of God. This young man by name Michael Wilson, has almost being killed several times. God saved him from a witchcraft family and Satan has not been happy ever since. On that Sunday morning, we hurried up to Church from Staten Island and were glad to be in the house of the Lord. Before Pastor Adeyeye commenced preaching, he gave a word of Knowledge about a young man who was withdrawing from college so he can work and make money. He commanded this young man by the word of the Lord to go back to college. Well, this young man was with us in church; that was Michael Wilson. He heard this word and he knew it was for him, but he did not know how this would happen.

However, the Lord placed what we were to do, on my heart. The Lord spoke to my heart during the service to take this young man to Valley Forge Christian College. Valley Forge Christian College in Pennsylvania is a school with more than 800 students. It takes at least a year of planning and tests and preparation to be admitted into this college. Their requirements are very stringent and the cost of this school is about $22,000 a year. God spoke to my heart to tell him to print the application, fill the application and take it with him on a trip to the college. On Monday, September 14, 2009, he humbly followed my instruction; although he told me later that he thought this was a crazy idea. How can you pack for college when you have not even turned in your application? He did not take the SAT tests. There was no financial aid application, no medical tests, and no health insurance. He had not been accepted. He had not chosen his classes. And it was very late in the school year. So many things needed to be done but we went anyway because we believed we heard God speak to us.

We drove down to Valley Forge Pennsylvania. When we got there they would not even talk to us about this matter, much less look at his application. I asked the Dean of Admissions for a minute of his time. And in just about 120 seconds God touched his heart. He took our case to his superiors and they told him to look at the application.

God quickened everyone that was there in the school that had anything to do with his enrollment. They moved in the love and power of God towards us. They processed the application and accepted him. They processed the financial aid and calculated his award to be nearly $20,000.00. They processed his health tests and insurance information. They assigned him his room. They ordered his transcripts. They assigned him his classes, took his picture, gave him his student ID, his username and password for the college Information Technology System. They ordered his MAC laptop for him because every student gets one. They gave him his meal tickets.

They connected him with some people that will help him catch up with the 4 weeks of classes he had missed.

All these were done in less than 10 hours. He moved in, and about 26 hours after he turned his application in, he started his classes! They told us they have not done anything like this in ten years.

Act on the word of God today and you will experience his hand. Never get so used to the man of God to the point where you take the word of God from his mouth for granted. The same God that did this for Michael Wilson will do it for you; as you act on His word today and all the days of your life in Jesus name. Glory be to God and all his wonderful works. —Brother M. Nwadiuko

God released me from Immigration Jail and I escaped Deportation!

The U.S. Immigration Enforcement came to my apartment in Brooklyn, New York in August, 2009. They took me to the Detention Center in Elizabeth, New Jersey with the intention of deporting me back to Nigeria on the next available flight. For the next three months, they tried all they could but were unable to deport me as a result of the fervent effective prayers of the saints. Pastor Festus Adeyeye came in there with his wife to pray for me and the entire congregation was consistently praying for me. I went into several days of fasting and praying asking God to foil the immigration plan of deporting me. To God be the glory! After about three months, they released me and also gave me papers to file for lawful employment. To God be all the glory for great things he has done. —Brother C. Nmorka

One-Month Mortgage Miracle

Luke 21:13 says, *"And it shall turn to you for a testimony."* I returned from a trip to Nigeria to discover that my tenant had stolen my identity. This was the beginning of an onslaught of financial woes that impinged on my house mortgage. Whenever I sent in my $2,300.00 monthly mortgage payment, the bank returned it adding fees. This pattern continued from January through July 2009. At one point, the bank advised me to get a lawyer to avoid bank foreclosure of my house.

However, I choose Christ as my righteous judge and I told the bank that I already had a lawyer. When the bank representative asked me who my lawyer was, I said "Jesus" and he hung up the phone. Strapped in debt and overwhelmed by the crisis, I "reported the matter in the court of Jesus" persistently in prayer. One day, during our month of "It shall turn into a testimony," the Holy Spirit prompted me to sow a financial seed of one-month mortgage to the church. Miraculously, after this financial seed and continuous prayer, a letter came from the bank with a reduction of my monthly mortgage payment and a supernatural cancellation of all my debt from January to July. To God be the glory. —Sister B. Agboola

My Landed Property was Stolen - and Restored

I was in a church service and Pastor Festus Adeyeye through a word of knowledge said, "There is somebody here whose landed property was taken from her;" he prayed prophetically that God will restore the land. I had purchased a piece of land a few years ago in Benin, Nigeria and had started building on it when suddenly there was serious contention among the children of the land owners. I did everything in court to regain my land but to no avail. Subsequently, they started utilizing the land for the production of cement blocks. However, the following Tuesday after the word of knowledge came through Pastor Adeyeye, my mother called me from Benin, Nigeria that she got a call that the dispute was resolved and the land and the property on it was given to me as the owner. They gave my mother the papers, which is in my name. Glory be to God! What the court of law couldn't do, God did through prayer. —Sister A. Imasuen

Deafness Healed

The first testimony of Glory Cloud 2009 in Baltimore, Maryland was given on Sunday evening, August 23, 2009 by Sister Bali. She had been an active participant of Glory Cloud '09, attending all of the daily events.

On Tuesday, under the ministration of Pastor Festus Adeyeye, she received her breakthrough. Sister Bali had being experiencing ongoing ear problem for 20 years, and found it hard to hear from her left ear. However, during the ministration, her case was specifically called out during a word of knowledge (prophesy) from Pastor Adeyeye. Pastor Adeyeye stated, "There is someone in the congregation whose left ear is being healed right now!" Shortly thereafter, Sister Bali heard a loud rushing noise in her ear, which was immediately followed by a loud pop, and from then onwards the clarity of her hearing was restored.

She exhorted the people saying, that if God could do it for her, he could definitely do it for them. To God be the Glory.

THE GREATEST PRAYER OF A LIFETIME

The greatest prayer of a lifetime is to be reconnected back to God in a living relationship. Relationship is the basis for asking. You cannot pray to a God whom you don't know and who does not know you. God wants to be intimate with you. This type of relationship is available to each one of us when we sincerely repent of our sins, and ask God's forgiveness, and receive His Son, Jesus, as our personal Lord and Savior. If you have never surrendered your life to God, or if you have turned away from God and you want to return to Him, now is the time. God is waiting for you. His arms are open wide to receive you. Just pray this simple prayer right now:

O Lord, be merciful to me, a sinner. I realize that I am a sinner. I need a savior and you are my savior. I repent of every sin, every wrongdoing, and I ask for your forgiveness. I receive Jesus Christ, Your only begotten Son, as my Lord and my Savior. I believe that Jesus went to the cross for me and paid the price for my salvation, and now I receive

Him into my heart. I declare that I am born again. I am a child of God. Old sins are gone, and I have a brand-new life in Christ in Jesus' name. Amen.

I WOULD *Love* TO HEAR FROM YOU!

I would love to hear from you, but even more than that, I would love to pray for you and write back to you. I hope you will let me know what you are believing God for, so we can join together in agreement and turn our faith loose for miracles!

Send your prayer requests to me by mail:

Festus Adeyeye
Adeyeye Evangelistic Ministries (AEM)
P.O Box 810
West Hempstead, NY 11552
e-mail: aboluade@aol.com
website: www.alccwinnershouse.org

ABOUT THE AUTHOR

Festus Adeyeye is the founding Pastor and the General Overseer of the Abundant Life Christian Ministries Worldwide. He is empowered with the Breakthrough Anointing and the mandate to liberate people from the oppression of darkness and ignorance.

Pastor Festus is a seasoned prophet, teacher and an Intercessor with the healing anointing. He is tremendously being used of God to raise fervent men and women that are taking communities, cities and nations for Christ.

He is a spiritual mentor to several pastors and he is also the founder of Possessing the Nations Ministerial Fellowship (PTNMF), a fellowship of ministers and church leaders with membership across the globe.

Pastor Festus is happily married to his "Best Friend," Pastor Anthonia, who also co-pastors with him at ALCC. They are blessed with Godly children.

www.ingramcontent.com/pod-product-compliance
Lightning Source LLC
Chambersburg PA
CBHW062009070426
42451CB00008BA/295